SILLY SCIENCE DISCARD

SILLY SCIENCE

Strange and Startling Projects to Amaze Your Family and Friends

Shar Levine and Leslie Johnstone

John Wiley & Sons, Inc.

New York • Chichester • Brisbane • Toronto • Singapore

Copyright © 1995 by Shar Levine and Leslie Johnstone
Published by John Wiley & Sons, Inc.
Illustrations © 1995 by Ed Shems

The publisher and the authors have made every reasonable effort to ensure that the experiments and activities in this book are safe when conducted as instructed but assume no responsibility for any damage caused or sustained while performing the experiments or activities in this book. Parents, guardians, and/or teachers should supervise young readers who undertake the experiments and activities in this book.

Library of Congress Cataloging-in-Publication Data
Levine, Shar.
     Silly science: strange and startling projects to amaze your family and friends/Shar Levine
  and Leslie Johnstone.
        p.   cm.
     Includes index.
     ISBN 0-471-11013-2 (pbk. : alk. paper)
        1. Science—Experiments—Juvenile literature.   2. Science—Experiments—Juvenile litera-
  ture.   3. Scientific recreations—Popular works.   4. Scientific recreations—Juvenile literature.
  [1. Science—Experiments.   2. Experiments.   3. Scientific recreations.   4. Science projects.
  5. Games.]   I. Johnstone, Leslie.   II. Title.
  Q164.L475   1995
  507.8—dc20   94-24698
                                                                                                      AC

Printed in the United States of America
10 9 8 7 6 5 4 3 2 1

To my family and friends—thanks for locking me in the office and making me coffee. Leslie—you kept me laughing and entertained—Can we do this again?

Shar

To my husband, Mark, my sons, Christopher and Nicholas, and my daughter, Megan, without whom this would not have been possible.
Thanks, Mom and Dad, for the expensive education.
Thank you, Shar, for asking me to do this and making it so much fun.

Leslie

~~~~~~~~~~~~~~~~~~~~~~~~~~~~~~~~~~~~~~~

Acknowledgments

The authors would like to thank Victoria Scudamore for her friendship and her chocolate, and for introducing us to each other.
Vicki, we love you!

And finally to Maurice Bridge—you sweet thing, you.

CONTENTS

INTRODUCTION

Science should be fun! That's why we've put together this collection of the silliest science experiments around. The experiments in this book are not meant to have any practical purpose. But that doesn't mean they are pointless. Each experiment illustrates a scientific principle. As you work your way through these activities, you will discover how scientific facts and theories apply to seemingly useless experiments.

There are 28 different experiments in this book. Each experiment includes a list of materials, a series of easy-to-follow steps, an explanation of the scientific principle demonstrated, and a Did You Know? section that offers additional scientific facts and information on each topic. You should have everything you need to perform the experiments right in your own kitchen, so there is no need to buy special or expensive materials.

HOW TO USE THIS BOOK

Read through each activity before you begin. Gather all the materials before starting, and place them in the order that you will use them. Give yourself plenty of space to work. Science can be messy, so wear old clothes while doing the experiment and cover any surfaces with newspaper. Do not eat, drink, or taste any of the experiments. Keep your work area neat, and wash instruments and hands after performing all activities.

This book explains the most common results for each experiment, but if your results are different, see if you can figure out why. After completing an activity according to the directions, you may want to think of ways to change the activity. What might the results be if you perform the experiment slightly differently? Before you make any changes, ask an adult to approve the substitution.

Scientific discovery is not always the result of careful planning toward a certain end. Scientists often discover one thing while looking for something quite different. There is even a word for this: *serendipity*. When performing experiments, it is important to keep an open mind and to continue to search for answers.

These activities can be shared, too. Try them with a parent, sibling, or friend. Bring this book to school and share it with your classmates!

Chapter 1
Hockey Night
in Canada

Have you ever noticed that it is easier to skate on a warm day than on a very cold day? In fact, if you were to go skating when it is 40° below zero, you might not be able to glide at all. Here is an experiment that explains why. (By the way, 40° below zero is the same temperature in Celsius as it is in Fahrenheit!)

YOU WILL NEED

loaf pan

tap water

cookie sheet

2 chairs

2 bricks or wooden blocks

2 1-gallon (4-liter) plastic milk jugs with handles, filled one-fourth full with water and capped

fine wire at least 1 foot (30 cm) long

salt

WHAT TO DO

1. Fill the pan with about 1½ inches (3 cm) of tap water. Place the pan in the freezer and leave it there overnight.

2. On the following day, place the cookie sheet between two chairs.

3. Place a brick lengthwise at each end of the cookie sheet.

4. Remove the block of ice from its container by quickly dipping the outside of the container in warm water. Rest one end of the ice block on each brick.

5. Attach a milk jug to each end of the wire.

6. Drape the wire over the middle of the ice block, making sure the jugs are balanced on either side of the ice block. The jugs should not touch the cookie sheet.

7. The wire will gradually cut through the ice. When it reaches the cookie sheet, pick up the ice. Are there two pieces of ice or just one?

8. Try this experiment again with a fresh block of ice. This time sprinkle some salt where the wire touches the ice. Do you get the same result?

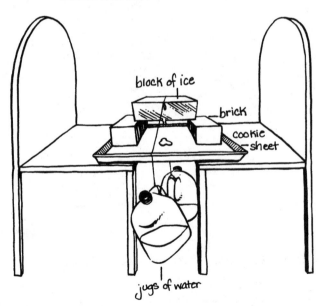

block of ice

brick

cookie sheet

jugs of water

4

WHAT HAPPENED

There was one piece of ice. By the time the wire had cut through the ice, the melted ice above it had refrozen. The wire exerted a large amount of **pressure** (force acting on an object) on the ice. Ice melts more easily if it is under pressure, so the wire melted the ice. When the wire moved into the ice block, the water above it was no longer under pressure, so it refroze. Like the wire, ice skates exert pressure on the ice, causing it to melt a little. Ice skates glide more easily on melted ice, but on a very cold day the water refreezes too quickly and the skates don't glide as well. When you sprinkled salt on the ice, the water did not refreeze, because salt water freezes at a lower temperature than freshwater.

DID YOU KNOW?

- If you look closely at the bottom of an ice skate blade, you will see that the blade has two parallel edges. Ice skates are designed to put the most pressure possible on a small surface. As you skate, the blades **thaw** (melt) a small amount of ice. You actually glide on a thin film of water. After you move away, the water refreezes.

- Salt is put on roads in winter to melt the ice and keep it from refreezing. Although it helps keep our roads from being slippery, salt can be damaging to the environment and to the metal bodies of automobiles.

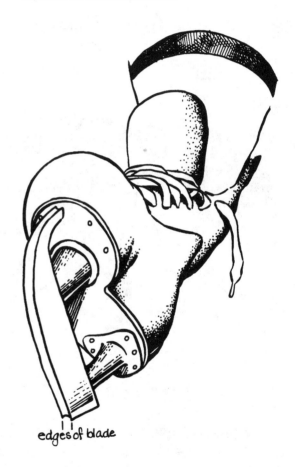

edges of blade

CHAPTER 2
GULLIVER'S EGGS

In *Gulliver's Travels* by Jonathan Swift, Gulliver found two countries at war over the right way to eat eggs. One country believed that people should eat the "little end" first, while the other country thought people should start with the "big end." This experiment will show you how to make either end of an egg point up, without using your hands!

YOU WILL NEED

2 identical egg cups
uncooked egg
hard-boiled egg

WHAT TO DO

1. Place one egg cup behind the other so that they touch. Put the uncooked egg into the cup closer to you.

2. Bend over the filled egg cup and blow downward as hard as you can onto the front edge of the cup.

3. Try the experiment again using a hard-boiled egg.

WHAT HAPPENED

The egg flipped from one cup to the other. The hard-boiled egg behaved the same way as the uncooked egg. The egg has a rough surface, so there is a gap between the side of the egg and the egg cup. When you blew air into this gap, it lifted the egg. The force that air puts on things is called **air pressure.** This very strong force can be used to move objects. Tools such as air hammers, and toys such as pump-up water guns, get their "muscle" from **compressed** air. The air in these tools and toys has been pressed or squeezed together into a smaller space, creating tremendous air pressure.

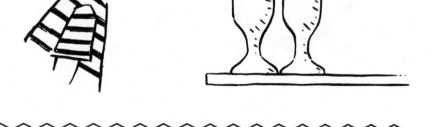

• Eggs can be very large or very small. The smallest bird's egg is that of the Jamaican hummingbird, which can be less than ⅖ inch (0.5 cm) long. The largest is that of the ostrich, which can be 6 to 8 inches (15 to 20 cm) long and can weigh about 3½ pounds (1.5 kg).

CHAPTER 3
SLAM-DANCING SPAGHETTI

If you want to liven up your dinner table with a colorful centerpiece, or if you're just looking for something to do on a rainy day, here's the experiment for you.

YOU WILL NEED

2 tall, thin glass jars or containers

tap water

food coloring

2 tablespoons (30 ml) baking soda

dried (not fresh) spaghetti and other types of pasta

½ cup (125 ml) vinegar

carbonated beverage

peanuts, popcorn, or raisins

WHAT TO DO

1. Fill one of the jars with warm water, leaving enough room for about 1 cup (250 ml) of liquid to be added.

2. Add a drop or two of food coloring to the water. Do not add so much food coloring that the water becomes dark.

3. Add the baking soda to the water.

4. Crush a handful of spaghetti and place it in the jar.

5. Pour the vinegar into the jar and observe what happens.

6. Repeat the experiment using different shaped pasta. Observe the effect that the shape or size of the pasta has.

7. Fill the other jar with a carbonated beverage, and use peanuts, popcorn, or raisins instead of pasta. Watch what happens.

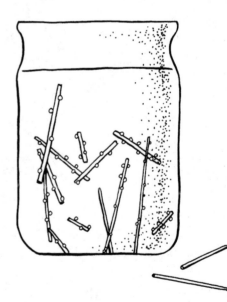

WHAT HAPPENED

A **chemical reaction** (a process whereby two or more substances are changed into another substance) occurred between the vinegar and the baking soda. This produced a gas called carbon dioxide. Bubbles of the gas collected on the pieces of spaghetti. Carbon dioxide is lighter than water, so the bubbles rose and the spaghetti hitched a ride. Smaller shapes of pasta move upward more easily; pasta with intricate shapes trap more bubbles and stay up longer. Carbonated beverages contain carbon dioxide, so the same thing happened to the food placed in the other container. The addition of carbon dioxide is called **carbonation**. This is what gives carbonated beverages their "fizz."

DID YOU KNOW?

- Vinegar is made from the **fermentation** (breakdown of plant material by yeast or bacteria) of liquids. Wine, cider, and malt liquor are some common beverages that can be made into vinegars. The chemical that gives vinegar its distinctive sour flavor is acetic acid. Vinegar contains about 1 part acetic acid for every 20 parts of liquid.

- One April Fool's Day, a television station showed the "harvest of spaghetti" from trees in Italy. Many people fell for the joke and believed that spaghetti grows on trees.

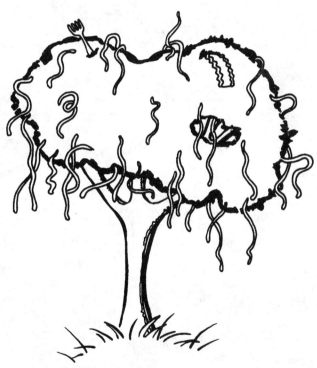

CHAPTER 4
PUMPING ALUMINUM

Before taking your empty aluminum cans and plastic soda pop bottles back to be recycled, here are two easy science experiments to perform with them. Ask a friend if he or she can crush a bottle without touching it, then amaze your friend with this trick.

YOU WILL NEED

measuring spoon

tap water

empty aluminum soda can

ruler

small saucepan

cookie sheet with rim

tongs or oven mitts

crushed ice

large plastic soda bottle with cap

adult helper

WHAT TO DO

Experiment 1

NOTE: To be performed with a stove and adult supervision.

1. Put 1 teaspoon (5 ml) of water in the empty soda can.

2. Put about 1 inch (2.5 cm) of water in the bottom of the saucepan, and place the can upright in the water.

3. Have an adult place the pot on a range and heat the can so that the water boils for several minutes and the can is filled with steam.

4. Place a cookie sheet filled with cold water on a counter close to the stove.

5. Have an adult use tongs to remove the can from the heat and immediately flip the can, top downward, into the pan of cold water. Watch what happens.

Experiment 2

1. Carefully place the crushed ice in the plastic soda bottle.

2. Screw on the cap, and leave the bottle in a warm place.

3. Watch what happens.

WHAT HAPPENED

In both experiments the can and the soda bottle crumpled inward. In the second experiment, the soda bottle bulged after sitting in a warm place for awhile. When air or water is heated, it **expands** (takes up more space). This increases the pressure inside its container, causing the container to bulge. When air or water is cooled, it **contracts** (takes up less space). This decreases the pressure inside its container, causing it to crumple. The outside air exerts about the same amount of pressure all the time. When the pressure inside the container is changed, the shape of the container also changes.

DID YOU KNOW?

- It takes more energy to make one aluminum can from aluminum ore than it does to make ten cans from recycled aluminum. An **ore** is a rock that can be processed to make a usable metal. Cans can be recycled almost completely, and the aluminum made from recycled cans is identical to the aluminum made from ore.

CHAPTER 5
MAKE IT SNAPPY

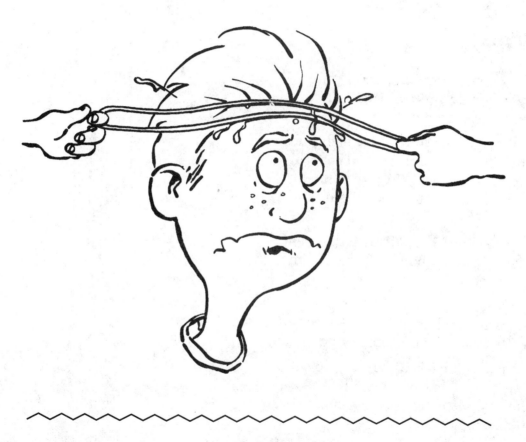

This science experiment makes you look incredibly silly. It works best when performed with several friends. This way you won't look ridiculous alone!

YOU WILL NEED

several sizes of rubber bands

large paper clip

ruler

coffee mug or other weight

blow dryer (to be used only by an adult)

adult helper

WHAT TO DO

1. Hold a rubber band across your upper lip or forehead, and make note of its temperature.

2. Remove it and quickly stretch and unstretch the rubber band several times. Then, hold it up to your lip or forehead again. Does it feel hot or cold?

3. Repeat steps 1 and 2 with different sizes of rubber bands. Observe any differences in temperature.

4. Suspend the rubber band from a doorknob and attach a paper clip to the bottom of the rubber band.

5. Attach a coffee mug to the clip so that the rubber band is stretched slightly. Measure the length of the rubber band.

6. Ask an adult helper to warm the stretched rubber band with a blow dryer. Watch what happens. (Measure the length of the rubber band again and calculate the distance it changed.)

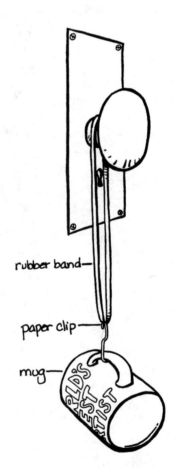

rubber band—

paper clip—

mug—

WHAT HAPPENED

The rubber band felt cool before you stretched it, then warmed up slightly after you stretched it. Stretching the rubber band rearranged its **molecules** (the smallest particles of a substance that keep the properties of that substance). The movement of the molecules created heat. Each time you stretched and unstretched the rubber band, you put energy into the rubber band, which was released as heat. The larger the rubber band, the more molecules it has and the more energy it can take in and release. The hot air from the blow dryer caused the rubber band to shrink, because adding heat energy rearranged the rubber molecules. As long as the rubber band is only stretched partway, it will become *shorter* when heated. That is what makes rubber bands interesting—most things expand when heated. When you turned the blow dryer off, the rubber band returned to its original shape. This effect is more noticeable in a rubber band because of its **elasticity** (the ability of a substance to return to its original shape after being deformed).

DID YOU KNOW?

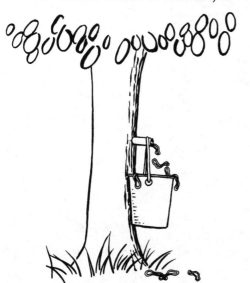

- Natural rubber is produced from **latex**, the sap of trees native to South America. A number of different plants can produce rubber, but most commercially produced rubber comes from the *Hevea* species of trees. **Synthetic** (man-made, not made by nature) rubber, which is made from petroleum oil, has very similar properties to natural rubber and is also quite common.

- Dandelion stems also contain an elastic material that, if collected and dried, acts much like rubber.

- The United States Postal Service uses the most rubber bands in the world.

CHAPTER 6
ROPE ROUNDUP

There are many tricks that you can perform using soap and water. Here's one to keep you busy while you're waiting for lunch or dinner.

YOU WILL NEED

shallow bowl

tap water

scissors

ruler

lightweight, noncotton string

toothpick

dishwashing liquid

sugar cube

WHAT TO DO

1. Fill the bowl with water.

2. Cut a 6-inch (15-cm) piece of string and tie the ends together.

3. Gently place the loop of string on the water so that it floats on the surface.

4. Dip the toothpick into a small amount of dishwashing liquid.

5. Dip the toothpick into the water in the center of the loop. Watch what happens.

6. Repeat the experiment with a loop of string that isn't tied. Watch what happens.

7. Repeat the experiment again, but dip the sugar cube into the center of the loop before you dip the toothpick. Watch what happens.

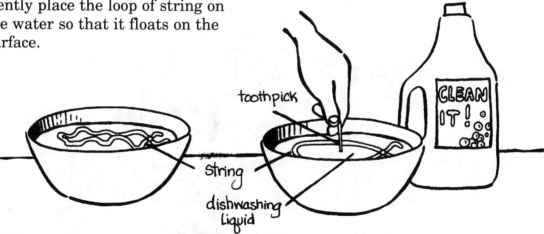

toothpick

string

dishwashing liquid

WHAT HAPPENED

When you dipped the toothpick into the water, the tied loop of string spread out into a perfect circle. Water molecules are attracted to each other, so those at the surface act like an elastic skin that can support lightweight objects. This characteristic of water is called **surface tension**. Dishwashing liquid contains oil and water molecules. The oil molecules broke the surface tension of the water inside the loop. This forced the water molecules to move away from the oil molecules, taking the string with them. The untied loop of string kept spreading out. When you dipped the sugar cube into the water, it **absorbed** (took in) some of the water on the surface. As the water molecules moved toward the sugar cube, the string did, too. When you dipped the toothpick in again, the water molecules and string moved away from the oil molecules again.

DID YOU KNOW?

- The next time you are at a pond, look for insects that are walking on water. Although the insects are heavier than the water and should sink, they do not. This is because of surface tension.

CHAPTER 7
IRON-POOR FOODS

Take a quick look through your cupboard and see if you have any iron-fortified foods. Many cereals and other products have added iron. Have you ever wondered what this means? Let's find out what kind of iron is in the cereal.

YOU WILL NEED

clear plastic bowl

a cereal labeled as containing "100% iron" or "reduced iron"

tap water

Teflon-coated bar magnet or a regular bar magnet wrapped in plastic wrap

timer

helper

WHAT TO DO

1. Fill the bowl with cereal and add enough water to cover the cereal.

2. Allow the cereal to become soggy.

3. Use the magnet to stir the cereal continually for about half an hour, taking turns with your helper.

4. Check the magnet from time to time.

WHAT HAPPENED

As you stirred the cereal, small black slivers began to form on the magnet. These tiny slivers, contained in many cereals, are a special form of a metal called iron. They are so small they are not normally noticed when the cereal is eaten; however, when collected with a magnet, they become visible. When you eat the cereal, the acids in your stomach react with the iron and change it into a form that can be easily digested. Your body uses the iron to make new blood. If you don't have enough iron in your diet, you could suffer from a medical condition called **anemia**, which would make you tire easily. You should not eat iron filings, though, as it would not be healthy to do so.

bar magnet

DID YOU KNOW?

- Cooking your food in pots and pans made from cast iron increases the amount of iron in your diet, because some of the iron from the pan is transferred to your food.

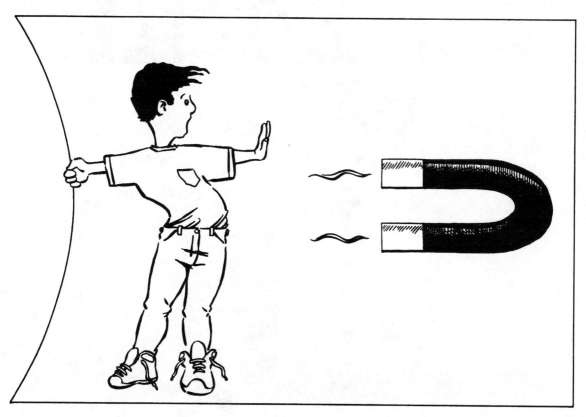

CHAPTER 8
GENIE IN A BOTTLE

Have you ever seen a ship in a bottle? How about a vegetable in a bottle? This experiment will take a while to complete, but the result will be worth it!

YOU WILL NEED

plant with baby fruits or vegetables, or fruit
  tree

jug or bottle

string or twine, or tape

adult helper

WHAT TO DO

NOTE: If you haven't planted a garden in
your backyard or don't have a fruit
tree, you can still perform this experiment. Buy a small vegetable plant
such as a squash, or grow a plant from
seed. Grow this plant indoors in a large
pot, following the steps below to perform the bottle trick.

1. Ask an adult helper to place a
small bud or baby vegetable into
the mouth of the bottle, being careful not to break the stem on the
plant or tree.

2. Secure the bottle to the plant by
tying or taping the bottle to the
stem, stalk, or branch.

3. Leave the bottle on the plant and
watch it grow.

4. Pick the bottled fruit when it has
filled the bottle.

WHAT HAPPENED

The fruit or vegetable continued to
grow inside the container because it
was still attached to the plant. The food
to help it grow was still supplied
through the stem. The vegetable or fruit
might even have taken the shape of the
bottle if it didn't have enough room to
grow into its usual shape.

DID YOU KNOW?

- There are special fruits grown in bottles that are used for expensive liqueurs.

- Specialty molds can be used to grow fruits and vegetables in the shape of faces or other objects. These molds are available through garden or mail order catalogs.

CHAPTER 9
SPONGESAURUS

Have you ever found a dinosaur bone? No? Well here's your chance to make one.

YOU WILL NEED

scissors

3 small kitchen sponges

2 buckets or sand pails

sand

table salt or Epsom salts

spoon

warm water

WHAT TO DO

1. Cut the sponges into the shape of bones.

2. Fill the first bucket halfway with sand.

3. Place the cutout sponges on top of the sand and cover them with more sand until they are completely buried.

4. Fill the second bucket about three-fourths full with warm water and stir in either table salt or Epsom salts. Keep adding salt and stirring until no more salt will dissolve.

5. Carefully pour the salt water onto the top of the sand.

6. Leave the bucket with the sand in a warm dry place and let the sand dry out completely. This may take several hours or overnight.

7. Dig out the sponges and dust them off.

water

sand

28

WHAT HAPPENED

The sponges turned hard and "bone-like." When the salt water was added to the sand, the salt particles filled in the spaces in the sponges. When the water **evaporated** (changed from a liquid to a gas), the salt remained in the spaces. The salt hardened, making the sponge hard like a bone. This is similar to what happens in the formation of some types of **fossils** (hardened remains or traces of plants or animals that lived long ago). Dissolved **minerals** (natural substances that are neither plant nor animal) go into the spaces in animal or plant material, where they dry and harden.

DID YOU KNOW?

- Fossil dinosaur bones are easily mistaken for rocks. One way to identify the bones is to touch them to your lower lip. The bones will stick to your lip and the rocks will fall off.

- The largest meat-eating dinosaur was the *Tyrannosaurus rex*. This giant was first discovered in 1900 at Hell Creek, Montana. A *T. rex* could be up to 45 feet (13.7 m) long and 20 feet (6 m) tall and have a skull 5½ feet (1.7 m) long.

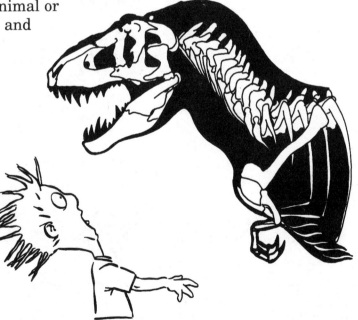

CHAPTER 10
BALLOONS AT THE BEACH

If you are bored with building sand castles, here is a fun and interesting experiment to try the next time you go to the beach.

YOU WILL NEED

rubber balloon
funnel
sand
tap water

WHAT TO DO

1. Stretch the neck of the balloon and wrap it around the funnel.

2. Partly fill the balloon with sand.

3. Add enough water to the balloon to cover the top of the sand but not to fill the balloon.

4. Tie a knot in the neck of the balloon.

5. Squeeze the balloon several times. Watch what happens.

WHAT HAPPENED

When you first squeezed the balloon, it moved easily. After a few squeezes, it became more and more difficult to squeeze. Sand grains are tiny mineral **crystals** (small, regularly shaped pieces) with several flat surfaces. When these flat surfaces are wet, they become **compacted** (packed together) in a pattern that prevents further movement.

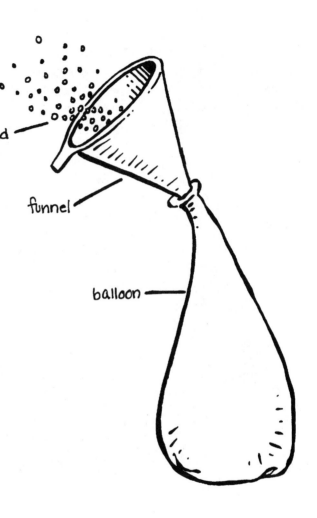

Sand

funnel

balloon

DID YOU KNOW?

- Sand castle builders use wet sand so that when the sand settles it keeps its shape better. Sand sticks together much better when it is wet. Dry sand would crumble and fall apart before the palace could be completed.

CHAPTER 11
WHERE'S THE BEEF?

Do you like going to sporting events and ordering a big, juicy hot dog? Do you ever wonder why it is juicy?

WARNING: This experiment may turn you into a vegetarian!

YOU WILL NEED

pen

paper

different kinds of hot dogs (such as chicken, all beef, regular, and tofu)

clear plastic wrap

kitchen scale

microwave-safe plates

knife (to be used only by an adult)

oven mitts

adult helper

WHAT TO DO

NOTE: To be performed with a microwave oven and adult supervision.

1. Create a table like the one shown, and enter the types of hot dogs in the first column.

2. Place each hot dog on a small piece of plastic wrap, weigh it, and enter the weight in the "before" column.

3. Place each hot dog on a small microwave-safe plate, and have an adult cut the hot dog into tiny pieces.

4. Place the individual plates in a microwave oven.

5. Have an adult cook the hot dogs until they stop shrinking (5 to 10 minutes on HIGH). Use caution if using a microwave because hot grease splatters. Do not leave the microwave unattended.

6. Have an adult use oven mitts to remove the plates from the oven. Allow the hot dogs to cool, then place each sample on clear plastic wrap.

7. Weigh each hot dog and record the weight in the "after" column.

8. To find out what percentage of water each hot dog contained, you need to do some simple math:

original weight – final weight = weight loss

weight loss ÷ original weight × 100 = percentage of water in hot dog

WHAT HAPPENED

The water evaporated from the hot dog, leaving mostly the meat and oil. Manufacturers vary the amount of water they put in their product. The water adds weight to the product, so less meat has to be put in. Hot dogs that are labeled "all beef" generally have a low percentage of added water. Hot dogs are made from different things. If you read the side of the package, you'll see the different kinds of meats, spices, and other ingredients. To give a hot dog its shape, all the ingredients are ground up and squeezed into a casing. This keeps the hot dog looking tubular and not flat like a hamburger.

DID YOU KNOW?

- People in North America have been drying meat for centuries. They hang strips of raw meat or fish, such as beef or salmon, to dry in the sun, and then store them for use during the long winter months. Dried meat is called jerky. Buy some and try it!

Type of Hot Dog	Weight Before	Weight After	Percentage of Water

CHAPTER 12
TITANIC

Why does a heavy iron ship float? Shouldn't something that heavy sink? Who was Archimedes, and what was his principle? For answers to these puzzling questions, read on.

YOU WILL NEED

pen

paper

container larger than a baby-food jar

tap water

empty baby-food jar with lid

nails

metric kitchen scale

large glass metric measuring cup

WHAT TO DO

1. Copy the table below onto a piece of paper.

2. Fill the container with water.

3. Fill the baby-food jar with nails, keeping track of the number of nails used. Screw the lid on tightly, and place the jar in the container

of water. If there are not enough nails in the jar to make it sink to the bottom of the container, remove the jar and add more nails until the jar sinks. Record the number of nails used in the first column of the table.

4. Remove the jar from the water, and weigh it on the scale. The weight shown on the scale is the **mass** of the jar, which represents the amount of material the jar and nails are made of. Record the weight (in grams) in the "mass" column.

5. Place the jar in the measuring cup, and fill the cup to the top mark with water. Remove the jar, and note the water level. Calculate the difference between the first water level, shown by the top mark, and

Number of Nails	Mass of Jar	Volume of Jar	Density of Jar	Floats/Sinks

the second water level, shown when the jar was removed. This number is the **volume** of the jar, the amount of space it occupies. Record the volume (in milliliters) on the table.

6. Divide the mass by the volume. The result is the amount of mass per unit of volume. This is the **density** of the jar and nails. Record the density (in grams per milliliter) on the table.

7. Place the jar and nails in the container of water, and record whether the jar floats or sinks in the last column of the table.

8. Remove two nails from the jar, then repeat steps 4 through 7. Continue removing nails two at a time and repeating the steps until the jar begins to float.

WHAT HAPPENED

When enough nails were removed from the baby-food jar, it floated. The number in the "volume" column stayed the same, even though the numbers in the "mass" and "density" columns changed. This is because the size of the jar remained the same; only its contents and their heaviness changed. The water also exerted an upward force that pushed against the jar. This upward force was equal to the weight of the water **displaced** (pushed out of position) by the jar. When the weight of the jar and the upward force were equal, the jar floated. At that point, the density of the jar was less than that of the water (1 gram per milliliter). This is the same principle that causes a heavy iron ship to float. It displaces so much water that the upward force is great.

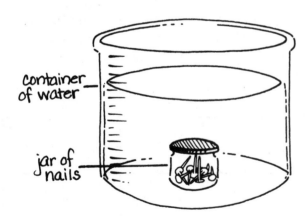

container of water

jar of nails

DID YOU KNOW?

- Archimedes (c. 287–212 B.C.), who lived in the ancient Greek city of Syracuse, was asked by the king to test a jeweler's honesty. The king wanted proof that his new crown was made from pure gold and not gold mixed with other, cheaper materials. How could Archimedes possibly prove this without damaging the crown? The answer came to Archimedes as he sat in his bath. He could measure the volume of the crown by measuring the weight of the water it displaced. Then, by calculating the density of the gold, he could prove the purity of the golden crown. He knew that the density of gold is greater than the density of gold mixed with other metals. Legend has it that Archimedes was so excited about his idea, which became the basis of what is now known as Archimedes' principle, that he jumped out of the bath and ran naked down the street, yelling "Eureka!" If he did the same thing today, he'd probably be arrested.

EUREKA!

CHAPTER 13
LESS FILLING

Have you ever gone bobbing for apples on Halloween? How about bobbing for soda cans at a family picnic? Are diet sodas less fattening because they weigh less than sugared colas?

YOU WILL NEED

kitchen food scale

an unopened can of regular carbonated soda

an unopened can of diet carbonated soda, the same brand as the regular soda

sugar

measuring spoon

sink or large cooler

tap water

WHAT TO DO

1. Weigh an unopened can of regular soda on a kitchen scale. Record the weight.

2. Weigh a can of diet soda and record the weight.

3. Leaving the diet soda on the scale, add sugar by the spoonful to the top of the can until the weight equals that of the regular soda. How many spoonfuls does it take?

4. Fill the sink or cooler with water.

5. Shake off the sugar and place both cans of soda into the water. Watch what happens.

WHAT HAPPENED

The diet soda weighed less than the regular soda. Adding sugar increased the weight of the diet soda. The diet soda floated, but the regular soda floated less or sank. Whether an object floats or sinks has more to do with its density than its weight. When carbonation is added to a liquid, the liquid has less density than water until other materials are added. The density of the carbonated beverages varied because of the types of sweetener added to them. The sugar syrup used in making the regular soda is heavier than the artificial sweetener (aspartame, like NutraSweet) used in the diet soda. This makes the regular soda more dense. Like the spaghetti noodles that hitched a ride on the bubbles of carbon dioxide gas in chapter 3, the cans of soda were lifted by carbonation. The difference in how well they floated was due to the type and amount of added sweetener.

DID YOU KNOW?

- One tablespoon (15 ml) of granulated sugar contains 48 calories. A **calorie** is a unit of measure for determining the amount of energy in food. The more calories a food has, the more energy it provides. If the calories are not "burned off" by activity, they are stored as fat in the body. Regular sodas are more fattening than diet sodas because they contain more calories. And although sugary beverages are heavier than diet drinks, it is their calories and not their weight that makes them fattening.

CHAPTER 14
GLUB

Many specialty toy stores sell a clear plastic cylinder filled with a gooey-looking substance that looks like an egg timer from another planet. Here's an easy way to make your own custom timer.

YOU WILL NEED

strong glue

2 identical small jars with lids (empty "junior size" baby-food jars work best)

nail

hammer

light corn syrup

spoon

food coloring

timer

adult helper

WHAT TO DO

1. Have an adult helper glue the tops of the two lids together.

2. When the glue on the lids has dried, have an adult poke a large hole through the lids using the nail and hammer. The hole should be about the size of your ring finger.

3. Fill one of the jars about three-fourths full with corn syrup. Stir in a few drops of food coloring to make the syrup your favorite color.

4. Screw the lid onto the jar. Turn the empty jar upside down and screw it tightly into the other lid. You now have one jar on top of the other.

5. Turn the jar with the liquid upside down so that it is on top of the empty jar. Measure the time it takes for the liquid to flow from the filled jar to the empty jar.

6. When the top jar is empty, repeat step 5.

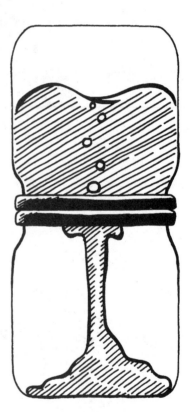

WHAT HAPPENED

Although the bottom jar appeared to be empty at the beginning of the experiment, it was actually filled with air. As the syrup in the top jar moved into the bottom jar, the air in the lower jar had to go somewhere to make room for the syrup. It moved into the top jar, and this was seen as air bubbles rising through the syrup. All liquids assume the shape of the container that they are poured into. Thick liquids such as syrup have a property called **viscosity** (resistance to flowing) that makes them take a long time to assume the shape of their container.

DID YOU KNOW?

• Viscous liquids flow faster if they are warmed up or more slowly if they are cooled down, because temperature affects viscosity.

• Viscous liquids are hard to compress. The harder you push on them, the less they give. This property makes them useful in such things as fluid-filled shock absorbers for automobiles.

45

CHAPTER 15
SAND PUZZLE

Many specialty gift and toy stores sell a puzzle that consists of a cylinder filled with colored powder and a ball bearing. The challenge of this puzzle is to make the ball bearing work its way through the powder from one end of the cylinder to the other. Here is a simple way to make your own custom puzzle (and the trick to solve it).

YOU WILL NEED

fine sand, corn meal, salt, or rice

powdered tempera paint

plastic cylinder with lid (an old bath salts container or plastic candy cylinder would be perfect)

small marble, round nut, or ball bearing much smaller than opening in cylinder

transparent tape

WHAT TO DO

1. Mix the sand with the tempera paint to give it color.

2. Fill the cylinder about three-fourths full with the colored sand.

3. Drop the marble into the cylinder.

4. Put the lid on the cylinder, and secure it with tape.

5. Try to move the marble from one end of the cylinder to the other.

NOTE: Turn the cylinder upside down so that the marble is on the bottom of the container. Lightly tap the bottom of the container on a table. Watch what happens!

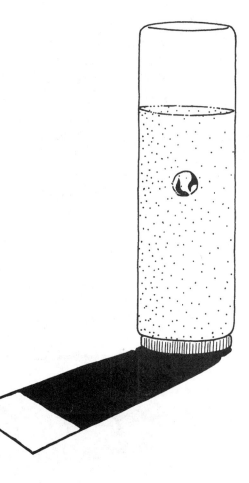

WHAT HAPPENED

The marble magically rose to the top of the cylinder! **Gravity** (force that pulls things toward large objects, like the Earth) caused the particles of sand to be compacted together. As you tapped the cylinder, the small particles of sand above the marble were loosened. This allowed them to move down and go around the marble. As they moved beneath the marble, they displaced it and pushed it upward. The weight of the marble compacted the particles below.

DID YOU KNOW?

• The large nuts in a can of mixed nuts will always rise to the top of the can. The same thing happens in nature when boulders rise to the surface of the ground. The loosening occurs when the ground freezes and thaws.

CHAPTER 16
CAVE-IN

Spelunkers are people who explore caves. If you aren't that adventuresome, you can build your own cave.

YOU WILL NEED

pencil or crayons

old shoe box without lid

aluminum foil

2 glasses

2 pieces of wool or cotton string

hot water

spoon

washing soda (available at a grocery store)

adult helper

WHAT TO DO

1. Draw a cave background on the inside bottom of the shoe box.

2. Line the outside and inside walls of the box with aluminum foil.

3. Turn the box on one long side. The faceup long side will be called the top of the box.

4. Have an adult use a pencil or other sharp object to poke two holes close together near each end of the top of the box.

5. Place a glass outside the box at each short end.

6. Thread each string in through one hole and out through the hole at the other end. The strings should be long enough to hang down slightly from the inside top of the box and reach the bottom of each glass. Do not put the strings in the glasses yet.

7. Fill the glasses with hot water, then stir washing soda into the glasses until no more soda will dissolve.

8. Place the strings in the glasses.

9. Leave the box for a few days in a dry place where it will not be disturbed.

WHAT HAPPENED

The string acted as a wick and drew up the washing soda and water mixture. The mixture dripped down the string and hardened as the water evaporated. These crystals of washing soda look like the stalagmites and stalactites in caves.

DID YOU KNOW?

- The stalagmites and stalactites in caves are formed in a similar way to the ones you made, except that in nature they are made from limestone. Limestone is a rock that is easily dissolved by rainwater seeping through the ceilings of caves. The dissolved minerals in the water drip from the ceiling and onto the floor. As the water evaporates, it leaves behind the mineral deposits to harden again. The deposits that grow downward from the ceiling are **stalactites**, while those that grow upward from the floor are **stalagmites**. This process takes hundreds of years, and the formations can be very beautiful.

CHAPTER 17
A-MAZE-ING POTATO

Here's a way to teach a potato to do a stupid vegetable trick. Somewhere in the back of your cupboard is a potato dying to help you out with this experiment.

YOU WILL NEED

scissors

shoe box or other small box with top

cardboard or paper

tape

small flowerpot

soil

sprouted potato

tap water

WHAT TO DO

1. Cut a small hole in one end of the shoe box.

2. Cut two or three pieces of cardboard or paper that are at least 1 inch (2.5 cm) shorter than the width of the box.

3. Use these pieces of cardboard to make partitions in the box. Tape the partitions into the box, attaching one end of each partition to the side of the box and leaving space at the other end. Tape the partitions in an alternating pattern to make a simple maze.

4. Fill the flowerpot with soil, and plant a sprouted section of potato in the soil. Water the plant.

5. Place the potted potato in the shoe box at the end opposite the hole. Close the box, place it in a window, and leave it there for several days. No peeking! You can open the box to water the plant if it becomes dry, but be sure to close the box immediately afterward.

6. When the sprout has come out of the hole at the end of the box, open the box.

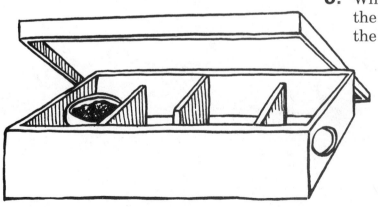

WHAT HAPPENED

The potato plant grew toward the light. Even though there was very little light entering the box, the sprout was able to find it and move toward it. The sprout is in a zigzag shape because it had to weave its way around the partitions. The sprout looks quite white because **chlorophyll** (the green coloring substance in plants) can only be formed when there is enough light. Plants need light to make food.

DID YOU KNOW?

- **Photosynthesis** is a process that occurs in all green plants. Green plants use the chlorophyll in their leaves and stems to make oxygen and sugar. They do this by taking in carbon dioxide from the air through their leaves and water from the soil through their roots.

- Plants are necessary for human and animal life, because they make oxygen. People and animals inhale oxygen and exhale carbon dioxide needed by plants.

CHAPTER 18
BUTTERED UP

I eat my peas with honey,

I've done it all my life.

It makes them taste quite funny,

but it keeps them on the knife.

—Children's nursery rhyme

Here's a silly experiment you can try at the dinner table that uses knives, forks, and spoons made from different materials.

YOU WILL NEED

3 similar pieces of cutlery made of different
   materials (steel, silver, plastic, or wood) but
   with similar lengths and thicknesses

mug

butter or hard margarine

small dried beans or peas

boiling water (to be handled only by an
   adult)

adult helper

WHAT TO DO

1. Stand the pieces of cutlery in the
   mug so that the handles stick out.

2. Using a small dab of butter or
   margarine, attach a bean or pea to
   the handle of each piece of cutlery
   at the same distance from the eat-
   ing end. The beans should all be at
   the same level.

3. Have an adult boil some water and
   pour it into the mug so that it
   comes up halfway between the bottom of the mug and the beans.
   Wait to see what happens.

WHAT HAPPENED

The butter melted and the beans fell
off the handles at different times. The
heat energy in the water was
conducted (transferred) up the handles to the butter. If your cutlery was
made of silver, stainless steel, or brass,
it conducted heat to the handle faster
than plastic or wood. The butter on the
metal handles melted faster because
metal is more conductive.

• There are materials called **superconductors** that conduct electricity with very little wasted energy. They must be used at very low temperatures. Many superconductors are made from **ceramics** (clay that has been hardened by baking at high temperatures). One group of ceramic chemicals, called **perovskites,** conducts electricity very well at temperatures around –288°F (–200°C). While this seems very cold, it is actually warmer than the temperature superconductors worked at in the past. Scientists are always trying to find superconductors that will work at higher temperatures, as very cold temperatures are more difficult and expensive to maintain. One day, superconductors may allow us to send inexpensive electricity over great distances.

CHAPTER 19
ELECTRIC PENCIL

Wouldn't it be great to have a pencil that did your homework for you? The good news is, here's a way to create an electric pencil. The bad news is, you still have to do your own homework!

YOU WILL NEED

knife (to be used only by an adult)

pencil without eraser

6-volt battery

3 pieces of electrical wire

2 alligator clips (optional)

flashlight bulb

adult helper

WHAT TO DO

1. Have an adult scrape away about ½ inch (1 cm) of the wood from both ends of a pencil so that there is this much pencil lead at each end.

2. Place the battery on one of its wide sides.

3. Attach a short piece of wire to each end of the pencil by wrapping the wire around the pencil lead or using an alligator clip. Connect the free end of one of these wires to the screwbase of the flashlight bulb. Connect the free end of the other wire to the positive terminal of the battery.

4. Use the third wire to connect the negative terminal of the battery to the metal tip of the light bulb.

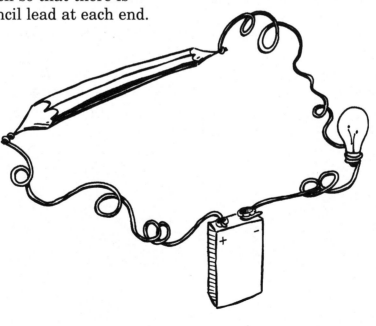

WHAT HAPPENED

The light bulb lit up. Electric energy was generated in the battery by a chemical reaction that caused a flow of tiny, negatively-charged particles called **electrons**. This flow of electric energy is called an **electric current**. To make the battery light the bulb, the current had to flow through a loop of conductive material called an **electric circuit**. Pencil lead is made from **graphite**, which is capable of conducting electricity. The electrons flowed through the wire from the negative terminal of the battery to the light bulb, then through the wire from the light bulb to one end of the graphite. The electrons then flowed through the graphite to the other end, then through the wire from the graphite to the positive terminal of the battery. The constant flow of electric current through this circuit caused the bulb to light up.

DID YOU KNOW?

- Graphite is a form of a natural, non-metallic substance called **carbon**. Another form of carbon is diamond. It is possible to make diamonds from graphite, but only if the graphite is put under great pressure. Diamonds occur in nature only under special conditions.

CHAPTER 20
SHAKE A LEG

How can you make a nylon stocking look as if a ghost is wearing it? This is a great experiment to do on Halloween or during a sleepover when scary stories are told.

YOU WILL NEED

piece of plastic wrap

nylon stocking (not a pair of panty hose)

timer

WHAT TO DO

1. Crumple the piece of plastic wrap, then hold it in one hand.

2. With your other hand, hold the nylon stocking by the toe against a wall.

3. Stroke the stocking from the toe down to the opening of the stocking with the crumpled plastic.

4. After 2 minutes of stroking, remove the stocking from the wall and hold it in the air. Watch what happens!

5. Bring the plastic wrap near the stocking, and watch what happens.

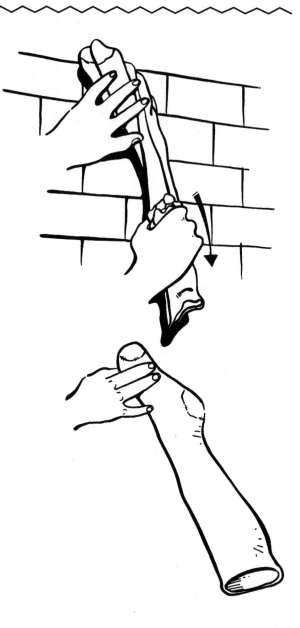

WHAT HAPPENED

A ghost leg seemed to fill the stocking when you pulled it away from the wall. When you brought the plastic wrap near the stocking again, the leg seemed to move toward the wrap, and the stocking made a zapping noise. You created an electric charge called **static electricity**, caused by an unequal number of negatively- and positively-charged particles. Both the stocking and the plastic wrap contained both types of particles at first, but rubbing the stocking with the plastic wrap moved the stocking's negatively-charged electrons into the plastic wrap. This made the stocking positively charged and the plastic wrap negatively charged. When all of the particles in a material are the same charge, the particles move away from each other. That is what happened to the particles in the stocking, so it opened up. This force is called **repulsion**. The particles in materials with opposite charges are drawn toward each other. That is why the positively-charged stocking was drawn toward the negatively-charged plastic wrap. This force is called **attraction**.

DID YOU KNOW?

- You can get a static charge by rubbing a balloon on your hair. You will get a stronger charge by rubbing the balloon on a cat and an even stronger charge by rubbing a balloon on a rabbit! This may be because electrons are more easily transferred from very fine fur than from hair.

- The amount of energy in electricity is measured in units called **volts**. The electric charge from static electricity can be as high as 10,000 volts!

CHAPTER 21
STATIC FIREFLIES

When you walk across a new carpet on a dry day, you can get a big shock. This is caused by static electricity. Here's a way to put static to good use.

YOU WILL NEED

screwdriver-type circuit tester (available at a
  hardware store)

Styrofoam or hard foam insulation

WHAT TO DO

NOTE: The results of this experiment may
be more visible in the dark.

1. Remove the small neon light
   from the handle of the circuit
   tester.

2. Hold one metal end of the light
   bulb in your hand, and rub the
   other end against the
   Styrofoam. Watch what happens.

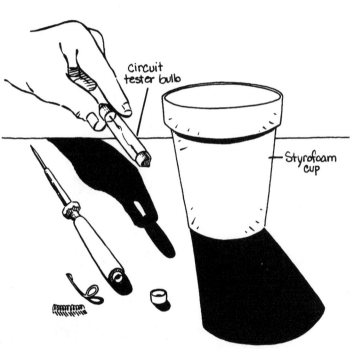

circuit
tester bulb

Styrofoam
cup

WHAT HAPPENED

The bulb lit up. Static electricity
built up as you rubbed the
Styrofoam. The electrons traveled
through the light bulb, causing it to
light up. The electrons then traveled
to your hand and into your body, but
you did not feel them because there
were not enough of them at one time.

DID YOU KNOW?

- If a large number of electrons go into your body at one time, you will feel a shocking sensation.

- **Neon**, which is used to make neon lights, is one of a special group of gases called **noble gases**. These gases don't usually react with other chemicals. Another common noble gas is **helium**, which is lighter than all other gases except hydrogen. It is used in balloons to make them float, because it is lighter than air.

CHAPTER 22
THE CRYING GAME

Boys and girls are equal, but they may not necessarily be the same! Here's one way to show a difference between boys and girls that's not X-rated. Try this experiment with your class. You won't be able to stop laughing.

YOU WILL NEED

girl, aged 10 or older

boy, aged 10 or older

tube of lipstick (Don't worry, boys. You don't have to put it on!)

WHAT TO DO

NOTE: For reasons that will become apparent after you have performed this experiment, it is necessary that the girl performs this experiment before the boy does.

1. Have a girl kneel on the floor. Make sure that her legs are close together and that she is not sitting back on her heels.

2. Instruct the girl to bend forward and place her elbows tightly against her knees, with her hands and palms extending outward, flat against the floor.

3. Stand a tube of lipstick at the tip of her longest fingers.

4. Without her moving her knees, have the girl go back to the kneeling position, clasp her hands behind her back above her waist, and keep them there.

5. Have her lean forward and try to knock the lipstick over with her nose, then return to the upright kneeling position, without using her hands.

6. Now, have a boy try it. No cheating!

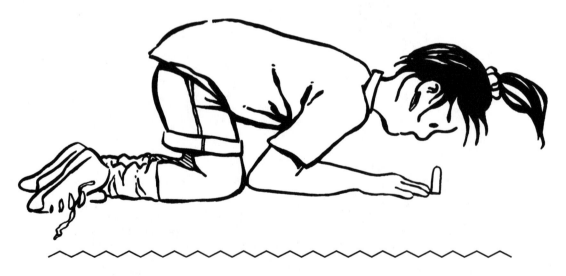

68

WHAT HAPPENED

Usually, boys will lose their balance and fall forward, but girls will be able to return to the upright kneeling position after knocking the lipstick over. The point on your body where your mass can be perfectly balanced by a supporting object, such as your knees, is called your **center of gravity**. Usually,

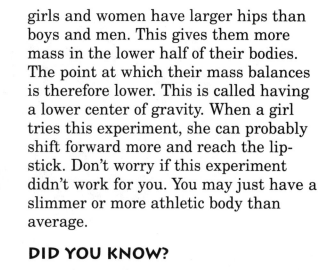

girls and women have larger hips than boys and men. This gives them more mass in the lower half of their bodies. The point at which their mass balances is therefore lower. This is called having a lower center of gravity. When a girl tries this experiment, she can probably shift forward more and reach the lipstick. Don't worry if this experiment didn't work for you. You may just have a slimmer or more athletic body than average.

DID YOU KNOW?

- Earthworms have both male and female parts in their bodies. There are no boy worms or girl worms; all worms are both sexes. Animals, like earthworms, that contain both male and female parts are called **hermaphrodites.**

Chapter 23
A Delicate Balance

Have you ever wondered how tightrope walkers keep their balance? Why do they carry that long pole? This experiment will help you to discover why.

YOU WILL NEED

salad fork

teaspoon

glass

wooden match (to be used only by an adult)

adult helper

WHAT TO DO

1. Holding the fork in one hand with the curves facing inward and the teaspoon in the other, lock the spoon between the tines of the fork so that the fork and spoon hold together.

2. Slide the wooden end of the match between the fork and spoon.

3. Use the long end of the match to balance the fork and spoon on the rim of the glass. This may take a few tries to find the right point.

4. Have an adult light the end of the match that extends over the rim of the glass. Allow the match to burn down.

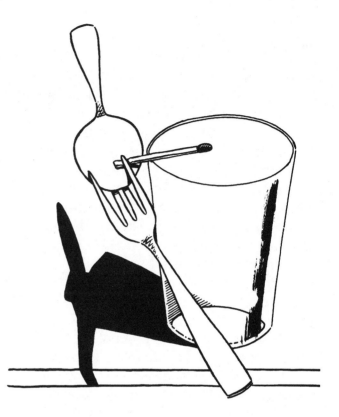

WHAT HAPPENED

The match burned until the flame reached the rim of the glass. Where the wood touched the glass, the heat from the burning match was transferred to the glass. The glass, being so much larger than the match, absorbed a lot of heat energy, keeping the temperature of the match below its **flashpoint** (the temperature it needs to reach in order to burn). The glass kept the wood from becoming hot enough to burn. The cutlery remained balanced because it extended from either side of the match. This gave the cutlery a lower center of gravity over the rim of the glass. Tightrope walkers use long poles for a similar reason. The pole gives them a greater mass on either side of their center of gravity. The extra mass means that if they move slightly to one side or the other, their center of gravity shifts only slightly.

DID YOU KNOW?

- The reason you don't fall over when you walk has to do with your ears. You have structures in your inner ear called **semicircular canals**. These fluid-filled tubes respond to changes in your position. **Vertigo** (dizziness) is a condition that occurs when these canals are damaged.

CHAPTER 24
FAST MONEY

Do you find money attractive? Does money seem to fly out of your wallet? Maybe there's a way to explain all this.

YOU WILL NEED

string

different kinds of paper money and checks—
American, Canadian, European

rubber cement or transparent tape

wire coat hanger

strong bar magnet or horseshoe magnet

WHAT TO DO

1. Attach a piece of string to the end of a bill by placing a dab of rubber cement on the bill, then pressing the string into the cement. Allow the cement to set.

2. Tie the other end of the string to the hanger. Suspend the hanger over an open space.

3. Hold a magnet close to the bill. Watch what happens.

4. Try this again, using a different bill. Observe any differences between the effects of the magnet on the bills.

5. When all bills have been tested, carefully remove the string and rub the dried rubber cement until it is loosened and removed.

WHAT HAPPENED

The bill probably moved toward the magnet. This is because some paper money contains small amounts of magnetic metals. These are probably iron salts, which are used in the dyes that color the paper. Magnetic inks are used to print the numbers that appear at the bottom of most checks. This helps banks to process checks.

• Governments take special steps to stop people from making their own money. Sometimes governments use special paper to print their bills. They also use special inks, so that they can tell whether the bills are real or not. If you hold certain European bills up to the light, you can see a colorless image pressed into the paper. This is called a **watermark**. The watermark is made during the papermaking process, and it is difficult to copy.

CHAPTER 25
FOILED AGAIN!

When a person likes to spend money, we sometimes say that money "burns a hole in his pocket." Here is an experiment that shows how that might happen if the person is wearing aluminum pants!

YOU WILL NEED

small clear plastic bowl

aluminum foil

penny

tap water

WHAT TO DO

1. Line the bottom of the bowl with foil.

2. Place the penny on top of the foil.

3. Pour enough water into the bowl to completely cover the foil and the penny.

4. Leave the bowl overnight. The next day, check to see what happened.

WHAT HAPPENED

The penny hasn't changed, but the aluminum foil has a hole in it where the penny was. This is because of a chemical process called **corrosion**, which causes metals to change color or break down when they are exposed to air or water. Often when two different metals come into contact with each other, a small electric current is produced that can cause one of the metals to break down, or corrode. The water is cloudy because it contains corroded aluminum particles.

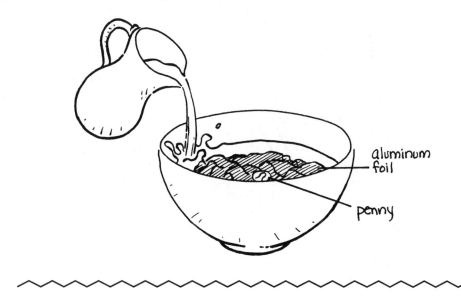

aluminum foil

penny

DID YOU KNOW?

- Until the early 1980s, pennies were made entirely of copper. Now they are made with a mixture of zinc and other metals and have a copper coating.

Chapter 26
A Very Dry Cell

This is a perfect experiment to try after you have mowed the lawn or when the leaves have started to fall off the trees. Instead of putting everything in a compost heap, you can make an "earth cell" battery. The battery you are about to make is called an "electrochemical cell."

YOU WILL NEED

wet leaves, soil, or compost

bucket

aluminum foil

sharpened pencil without eraser

two 10-inch (25-cm) pieces of electrical wire

multirange voltage tester capable of measuring less than 1 volt

WHAT TO DO

1. Put the wet leaves in the bucket.

2. Roll a piece of aluminum foil into a rod, and place one end of it in the leaves.

3. Place the unsharpened end of the pencil in the same container, near but not touching the aluminum foil.

4. Wrap one end of one of the wires around the free end of the aluminum foil. Wrap one end of the other wire around the pencil lead.

5. Connect the free ends of the wires to the voltage tester according to the directions that came with the tester. See what voltage was produced.

6. Look at the tester.

rolled foil

pencil lead

wet leaves

WHAT HAPPENED

You have created an **electrochemical cell** (a device that causes the chemical production of electricity) that can produce up to 0.3 volts of electricity. This type of cell battery consists of two parts. The wet leaves, soil, or compost is the **electrolyte** (a liquid mixture that allows electrons to flow through it). The aluminum foil and the pencil lead, which is made of graphite, are the two **electrodes** (materials capable of producing electricity between each other). Because the electrodes are made of different materials, a chemical reaction occurs between them through the electrolyte. This draws electrons from one electrode to the other through the wires that are connected to the voltage tester. The tester measures the amount of voltage that can be produced by the two electrodes.

DID YOU KNOW?

• An electric eel can produce over 400 volts of electricity. This is enough to zap its prey or protect the eel from its predators. The eel also uses electricity to locate its food.

CHAPTER 27

SMOKE GETS IN YOUR IVY

Here's a science experiment that's also art.

YOU WILL NEED

grease or petroleum jelly

2 smooth, round glass bottles with lids

cold tap water

matches (to be used only by an adult)

candle

leaf

newspaper

colored or white paper

adult helper

WHAT TO DO

1. Spread a thin layer of grease on the outside of one of the bottles.

2. Fill the bottle with cold water, and cap it.

3. Have an adult light the candle and hold the bottle over the flame. This will cover the bottle with **soot** (the black powder that colors smoke). Wait till the bottle cools a little before you touch it.

4. Place a leaf, bumpy side up, on a sheet of newspaper, then roll the bottle over the leaf. This will cover the leaf with soot.

5. Place the leaf, soot side up, on a clean sheet of newspaper. Place the colored or white sheet of paper over the leaf.

6. Roll the other, clean, bottle over the paper to make a print.

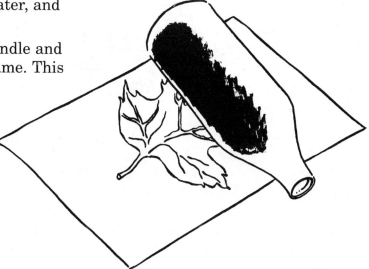

WHAT HAPPENED

When candles burn, they produce fine particles of carbon, which go into the air as soot. The grease on the bottle trapped the soot. This soot was then used to make a print from the leaf.

DID YOU KNOW?

- Gasoline used to power cars causes more **pollution** (poisoning of the environment by man-made substances) than natural gas, propane, or alcohol because it produces more carbon when burned. Using a different kind of fuel to run your car will cut down on air pollution.

CHAPTER 28
COFFEE TO GO

Many people have wondered if there is another way to get rid of Styrofoam containers besides just dumping them in landfills. **Environmentalists** (people who care about preserving nature) are concerned about the amount of Styrofoam in landfills, because these containers do not **biodegrade** (break down into harmless substances). Here is an impractical way of eliminating Styrofoam.

WHAT YOU NEED

⅓ cup (100 ml) nail polish remover with
 acetone (to be used only by an adult)

small glass bowl or metal container

Styrofoam cup

plastic knife or spoon

disposable dish

Styrofoam packing chips

adult helper

WHAT TO DO

WARNING: This experiment must be performed in a well-ventilated area
and away from open flames.
Have an adult supervise this
activity. Do not eat or drink any
of the liquids. Wash hands after
handling the materials used.

1. Have an adult pour the nail polish
   remover into the bowl.

2. Break the Styrofoam cup into
   pieces, and place the pieces in the
   bowl. Watch what happens.

3. Have an adult use a plastic knife
   to remove the guck from the bottom of the bowl. Place the guck in
   a disposable dish and allow it to
   harden.

4. Repeat the experiment, using the
   packing chips. Observe any difference in the amount of time they
   take to dissolve.

Styrofoam
cup

WHAT HAPPENED

The chemicals in the nail polish remover broke apart some of the connections between the chemicals in the Styrofoam. It did not completely dissolve the Styrofoam, so you were left with the guck. Eventually, when the remover evaporated, the guck hardened.

DID YOU KNOW?

- It is possible to turn a Styrofoam cup inside out without breaking it. After you have finished a warm cup of cocoa, have an adult rinse the cup out with boiling water. Turn the cup upside down, then use both your thumbs to gently push the bottom rim inward. Continue doing this until you have turned the cup inside out.

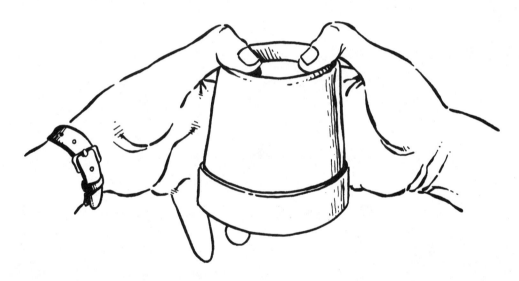

GLOSSARY

absorb To take in a substance, such as water.

air pressure The force that air puts on things.

anemia A medical condition caused by a lack of iron in the blood which makes people tire easily.

attraction The force by which particles with opposite charges are drawn toward each other.

biodegrade To break down into harmless substances.

calorie The unit of measure for determining the amount of energy in food.

carbon A nonmetallic substance that exists in nature as graphite or diamonds.

carbonation The addition of carbon dioxide to such things as soft drinks.

center of gravity The point in an object where its mass can be perfectly balanced by a supporting object.

ceramics Clay that has been hardened by baking at high temperatures.

chemical reaction A process that changes substances into other different substances.

chlorophyll The green colored substance in plants that is necessary for photosynthesis.

compact To pack together.

compressed Pressed or squeezed together.

conduct To transfer heat or electricity in solid objects.

contract To take up less space.

corrosion The chemical process that causes metals to change color or break down when they are exposed to air or water.

crystal A small, regularly shaped piece of a solid.

density The amount of mass in an object per unit of volume.

displace   To push out of position.

elasticity   The ability of a substance to return to its original shape after being deformed.

electric circuit   A loop of conductive material through which an electric current can flow.

electric current   A flow of electric energy.

electrochemical cell   A device consisting of two electrodes and an electrolyte, which causes the chemical production of electricity.

electrode   One of two materials capable of producing electricity between each other in an electrochemical cell.

electrolyte   A liquid mixture that allows electrons to flow through it.

electron   A tiny, negatively-charged particle.

environmentalist   A person who cares about preserving nature.

evaporate   To change from a liquid to a gas.

expand   To take up more space.

fermentation   A chemical process involving the use of yeast or bacteria to break down plant material.

flashpoint   The temperature a substance must reach in order to burn.

fossil   The hardened remains or traces of a plant or animal that lived long ago.

graphite   A form of carbon that is black, soft, and greasy feeling.

gravity   The force that pulls things toward large objects, like the Earth.

helium   A noble gas that is lighter than all other gases except hydrogen and is used in balloons to make them float.

hermaphrodite   An animal that has both male and female parts.

latex   The sap of trees from which natural rubber is made.

mass   The amount of material that an object is made of.

mineral   A natural substance, neither plant nor animal.

molecules   The smallest particles of a substance that keep the properties of that substance.

neon   A noble gas that is used in neon lights.

noble gases A group of gases that do not usually react with other substances. The group includes helium, neon, argon, krypton, radon, and xenon.

ore A rock that can be processed to make a usable metal.

perovskites A group of ceramic chemicals that conduct electricity at temperatures around $-288°F$ $(-200°C)$.

photosynthesis The chemical process in green plants whereby the plants use chlorophyll and sunlight to change carbon dioxide and water into oxygen and sugar.

pollution The poisoning of the environment by man-made substances.

pressure The force acting on an object.

repulsion The force by which particles with the same charge move away from each other.

semicircular canals Small, fluid-filled structures in the inner ear that are used to detect changes in position and enable a person to balance.

soot The black powder that colors smoke.

spelunkers People who explore caves.

stalactites Limestone deposits that grow downward from the ceilings of caves.

stalagmites Limestone deposits that grow upward from floors of caves.

static electricity An electric charge caused by an unequal number of negative and positive particles on an object.

superconductor A material that conducts electricity with very little wasted energy.

surface tension The attraction between water molecules that causes the surface of the water to act like an elastic skin to support lightweight objects.

synthetic Man-made, not made by nature.

thaw To melt.

vertigo A feeling of dizziness that can be caused by damage to the inner ear.

viscosity The property of some thick liquids that causes them to resist flowing.

volt   The unit of measure used to determine the amount of energy in electricity.

volume   The amount of space an object occupies.

watermark   A colorless image pressed into paper during the papermaking process.

INDEX

READER REPLY FORM

YOU CAN HELP US WRITE A BOOK!

Do you wonder how we come up with all these silly experiments? Some of them come through hard work, some happen by accident, and some are from our friends and coworkers. Here's your chance to become an author. Have you got a favorite useless experiment or science fact? Have you done a science experiment in your classroom that made everyone say "wow!"? You can send us your favorite project and, if our editors are still speaking to us, we'll write a book with your special activity.

HERE'S HOW IT WORKS:

1. Try out your science experiment with an adult family member or a teacher.
2. Write what you did on a copy of the "Silly Experiment" form.
3. Have an adult cosign the form.
4. Mail the form to us:

John Wiley & Sons Inc.
605 Third Ave.
New York, New York 10158-0012

Attention: Shar Levine / Leslie Johnstone
In care of Kate Bradford

SILLY EXPERIMENT

Name of Experiment _____

Materials You Need

_____

_____

_____

_____

_____

_____

What to Do

1. _____
2. _____
3. _____
4. _____
5. _____
6. _____
7. _____
8. _____
9. _____
10. _____

What Happened

_____

_____

_____

_____

_____

Experimenter's Name _____ Age _____

Address_____

City _____State/Province _____Country _____

ZIP Code/Postal Code _____ Phone Number (___) _____